Lace:
Australian Wildflowers
in Point Ground

Elwyn Kenn

Kangaroo Press

Contents

Bibliography

Practical

KENN, ELWYN, *Point Ground Patterns from Australia*, Kangaroo Press, 1986

CHANNER, C.C., & WALLER, M., *Lacemaking Point Ground*, Dryad Press, 1985

NOTTINGHAM, PAMELA, *The Technique of Bucks Point Lace*, B.T. Batsford, 1982

COOK, BRIDGET M., *Practical Skills in Bobbin Lace*, B.T. Batsford, 1987

Historical

SIMEON, MARGARET, *The History of Lace*, Stainer and Bell, 1979

LEVEY, SANTINA M., *Lace—A History*, Victoria & Albert Museum in association with W.S. Maney & Son Ltd, 1983

Front cover: Bower Plant mat with Australian wildflowers and lace bobbins

© Elwyn Kenn 1990

First published in 1990 by Kangaroo Press Pty Ltd
3 Whitehall Road (P.O. Box 75), Kenthurst NSW 2156
Typeset by G.T. Setters Pty Limited, Sydney
Printed in Hong Kong by Colorcraft Ltd

ISBN 0 86417 288 5

Introduction

The art of making bobbin lace is challenging, but it is a great deal of fun—enjoyment is the key.

In this, my second book of Point Ground patterns based on Australian flora, I have introduced the lacemaker to new techniques including floral lace.

A sound knowledge of bobbin lacemaking is assumed; this is not a book for absolute beginners. The lacemaker should be familiar with stitches and techniques such as whole stitch (also called cloth or linen stitch), half stitch, working a footside, and the use of a gimp thread.

The patterns are progressive, beginning with the basic stitches, and are designed to introduce new techniques as you work.

The patterns were worked with the threads stated, but the prickings may be enlarged or reduced to accommodate coarser or finer threads. With experimentation ideas will develop. Use a soft coloured silk thread or a bright cotton as well as the traditional white thread.

I hope this book will help and guide you and add a new challenge.

Symbols used in diagrams

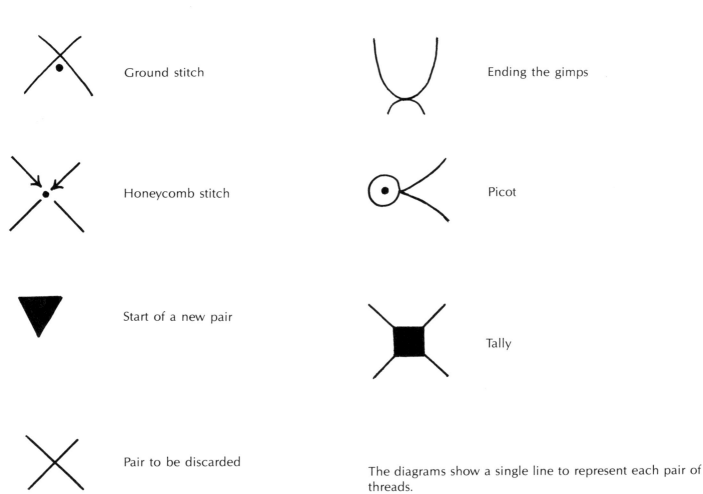

Ground stitch

Honeycomb stitch

Start of a new pair

Pair to be discarded

Ending the gimps

Picot

Tally

The diagrams show a single line to represent each pair of threads.

Lillypilly
Acmena smithii

- 13 pairs of bobbins wound with Madeira No. 50, DMC No. 50 or Brok 100.
- 1 gimp pair wound with Perle No. 8.

Ground stitch Called Buckingham Point, Tulle or Lille Ground. This is the basic stitch for these laces. It is worked: half stitch and twist each pair twice (or cross and 3 twists). A pin is put between the pairs. Pins in point ground are not covered (Fig. 1).

Fig. 1

Fig. 2

To begin along a straight edge Hang 2 pairs on a pin at A. Twist the pairs on each side of the pin 3 times (Fig. 2).

Place 2 pins at B and hang 1 pair on each pin. *Note* The pinholes at B are not marked on the pricking.

These pairs are the footside passives and are untwisted throughout.

An easier and neater join is achieved when the 2 passives are hung on separate pins (Fig. 3).

Hang 2 pairs on the ground pins C and D. Twist the pairs each side of pins C and D 3 times and leave.

Return to A and work a whole stitch then twist each pair 3 times. With the left-hand pair from A work in whole stitch through the 2 passive pairs, give 3 twists and put a pin at E to the right of this pair (Fig. 4).

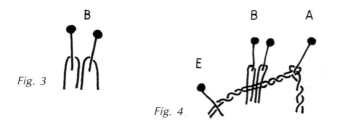

Fig. 3

Fig. 4

Footside and catchpin To work the catchpin a ground stitch is worked with the pair from E and the right-hand pair from C. No pin is placed under this ground stitch as pin E is already in place.

Take the 4th pair from the footside and work in whole stitch through the 2 passive pairs towards the footside edge.

Twist the workers 3 times and put a pin at F to the left of the twisted pair. Work a whole stitch with the footside pair, then twist each pair 3 times.

With the left-hand pair from F work back through the 2 passive pairs in whole stitch. Twist the workers 3 times and put a pin at G to the right of this pair.

The pair at G is now ready to work the next catchpin.

Catchpins are worked where the footside meets the ground.

To work the ground With the right-hand pair from D and the left-hand pair from C work a ground stitch and put a pin at H. Ground stitches are worked in diagonal rows and may be worked to or from the footside. They are worked in blocks as far as possible.

Work the next ground stitch towards the footside then the catchpin at G. The footside is worked as before.

Gimp Hang the gimp pair on a temporary pin above J. Place temporary pins on each side of the gimp and hang 1 pair of bobbins on each pin (Fig. 5).

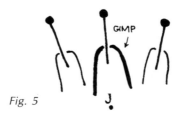

Fig. 5

The gimp thread is passed through pairs in either direction by lifting the left-hand bobbin of each pair. The pairs are then twisted twice ready to work a honeycomb stitch.

A gimp thread is enclosed with 3 twists between the gimp and a ground stitch, 2 twists between the gimp and a honeycomb stitch and 1 or 2 twists between the gimp and whole stitch. Generally there are no twists between 2 gimp threads which lie together.

Honeycomb stitch A honeycomb stitch is worked at J with the pairs from the temporary pins.

Honeycomb stitch is worked: half stitch and twist each pair once (or cross and 2 twists), pin, cover the pin with a cross and 2 twists. Remove the temporary pins and ease the threads into place.

The gimp is passed through the left-hand pair from D and given 2 twists ready to work the next honeycomb stitch.

Now work the honeycomb stitch with the right-hand pair from J and the left-hand pair from D.

Hang 1 pair on a pin for the headside passives. Normally there are 2 passives at the headside. The 2nd passive in this pattern comes from the false picot.

False picots   False picots are used to introduce new pairs at the headside, either at the start of the work or when extra pairs are added at the corner. They are worked as follows: hang 2 pairs on a pin. Twist the pairs each side of the pin 3 times. Work a whole stitch then twist each pair twice. One pair is then worked through the headside passives into the ground, the other pair becomes the 2nd headside passive (Fig. 6).

FALSE PICOT

GIMP

Fig. 6

After the workers have passed through the headside passives, give 2 twists, pass the gimp through then give 2 more twists ready to work a honeycomb stitch.

Crossing the gimps   Complete the first honeycomb ring and cross the gimps right over left.

Gimp threads are usually crossed right over left or left over right and continued in this way throughout the pattern.

Sometimes the design calls for a breaking of this rule as it is the appearance of the lace which is important.

Work the next honeycomb ring and the ground as far as possible.

Picot   Using the pair to work the first picot, give 2 twists then work in whole stitch through the 2 headside passive pairs. Twist the workers 6 times and make a double picot (Fig. 7). Twist 3 times then pull very gently but firmly so the threads will twist together around the pin. Work in whole stitch back through the passives, then twist the workers 3 times ready to work the next ground stitch.

There can be a variation in the number of twists used for picots. The picot must remain twisted and not split when the pin is removed. The number of twists will depend on the thickness of the thread and the size of the pin.

Work next block of ground and picots then complete pattern working honeycomb rings and ground as before.

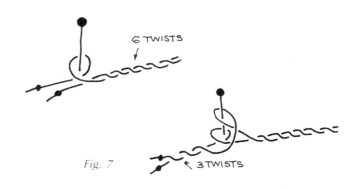

6 TWISTS

3 TWISTS

Fig. 7

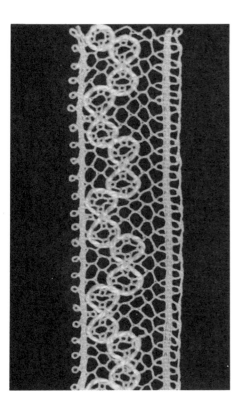

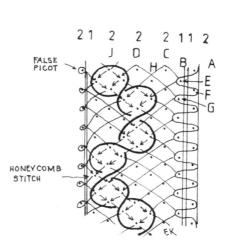

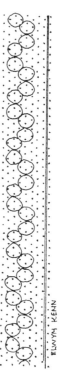

Golden Rain Wattle
Acacia prominens

- 14 pairs—Brok 120 or Madeira 'Tanne' No. 80.
- 1 gimp pair—Perle No. 12.

To begin along a straight edge This pattern shows an alternative method for beginning along a straight edge.

Tallies in the ground Tallies are worked instead of ground stitches. Work in diagonal rows until the tally is reached.

There are several ways to work a tally—this is only one method. Take the third thread from the left and use this to weave under the 2nd and over the 1st. Bring the thread back under the 1st, over the 2nd, under the 3rd, back over the 3rd to the original position. Tension, keeping the outside threads taut as these threads control the width.

Continue to weave in this way until the tally is completed. Do not allow the weaver to tighten (Fig. 8). On completion the weaver is the 2nd thread from the right.

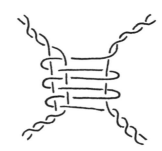

Fig. 8

Twist the 2 left-hand threads and the 2 right-hand threads 3 times and place a temporary pin between the threads to support them. Also support the weaver as any tension on this thread will destroy the shape of the tally.

It is important at the end of the tally that the pair without the weaver (the left-hand pair from the tally) is worked into the ground before working the right-hand pair which contains the weaver.

6 pin honeycomb ring In this pattern a 6 pin honeycomb ring is introduced. The 6 stitches inside the gimp are honeycomb stitches. Work in the direction of the arrows in the working diagram.

Fingers of gimp worked through the ground There are various ways of working fingers in the ground. The method of working depends on the particular effect required.

A. The gimp is passed through the pairs and ground stitches are worked. Use this method if a continuity of ground stitches is required.

B. If the fingers are to represent leaves, a more rounded appearance is needed, achieved by working a honeycomb stitch at the tip of the leaf. After passing the gimp through the pairs, 2 twists are given to the pairs at the tip of the leaf and a honeycomb stitch is worked. The other pair or pairs of the leaf are not twisted after the gimp. Work a whole stitch, no twists, then pass the gimp through. Twist the pairs 3 times ready to continue in ground stitch (Fig. 9).

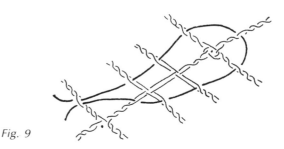

Fig. 9

For a wider leaf, 2 honeycomb stitches are worked in the same way at the tip of the leaf.

Working with a gimp loop The leaves in this pattern cannot be worked in a straightforward manner.

After crossing the gimps below the 6 pin honeycomb ring pass the gimp thread to the right through 4 pairs. Give 2 twists to the 3rd and 4th pairs ready to work the honeycomb stitches of the leaf.

Make a big loop with the gimp and pin to the pillow. The pairs with the twists work the leaf so these pairs are laid aside to the right. The gimp then goes to the left through the next 2 pairs. Give these 2 pairs 3 twists each then pass the 2 gimps through the next pair to the left (the pair from the honeycomb stitch below the ring) and give 3 twists.

The 2 ground stitches are now worked. The right-hand pair from the last ground stitch is used to work the leaf. Pass one bobbin under and the other bobbin over the gimp loop. Give 2 twists and work the 2 honeycomb stitches of the leaf.

The 3 pairs from the leaf are then passed under and over the gimp loop as before and twisted 3 times ready to work ground stitches. The gimp is then pulled gently into position.

Continue the ground. The 2nd and 3rd leaves are worked in the same manner.

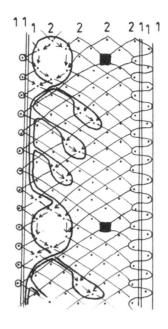

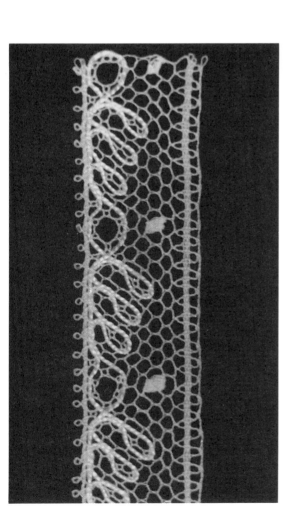

Small-leaved Boronia
Boronia microphylla

- 29 pairs—Brok 120 or Madeira 'Tanne' No. 80.
- 2 gimp pairs—Perle No. 12.

To begin on an angle   Hang 2 pairs on a pin at A. Twist the pairs on each side of the pin 3 times. Work whole stitch with the 2 pairs, then twist each pair 3 times (Fig. 10).

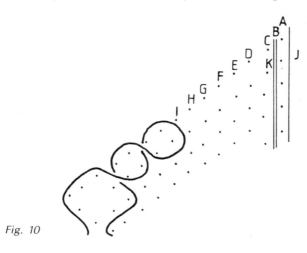

Fig. 10

Place 2 pins at B and hang 1 pair on each pin. *Note* The pinholes at B are not marked on the pricking. These are the footside passives and are untwisted throughout.

At A leave the right-hand pair, take the left-hand pair and work in whole stitch through the 2 passive pairs from B. Twist the workers 3 times and put a pin at C, to the right of the twisted pair (Fig. 11).

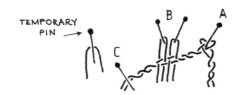

TEMPORARY PIN →

Fig. 11

Hang 1 pair on a temporary pin above C. It is a good idea to use pins with coloured heads for temporary pins as they are easily identified. Work a ground stitch with this pair and the pair left hanging at C for the catchpin. The pin is to the right of both pairs. Hang 1 pair on each pin from D to I for the ground stitches. Take the 5th pair from the footside and work a ground stitch with the pair from D. Support the 4 bobbins which have worked the stitch, take

out the pin and replace between the pairs. With the left-hand pair from the stitch just worked, and the next pair to the left from E, work a ground stitch, taking the pin out and replacing as before.

Continue to work ground stitches in the same manner at each pinhole to I. Remove the temporary pin above C and ease the pair down into place. If all the ground stitches have been worked correctly with 3 twists, the extreme left thread travels across the work from the footside. Check by carefully pulling the left-hand bobbin.

Footside and catchpin   Take the 4th pair from the footside and work in whole stitch through the 2 passive pairs towards the footside edge. Twist the workers 3 times and put a pin at J, to the left of the twisted pair. Work whole stitch with the footside edge pair, then twist each pair 3 times.

With the left-hand pair from J work back through the 2 passive pairs in whole stitch. Twist the workers 3 times and put a pin at K to the right of this pair.

The pair at K is now ready to work the next catchpin. Work the block of ground, honeycomb rings and the tally.

Whole stitch diamond   1 twist is given to each pair after the gimp has been passed through and before working the diamond.

In this pattern we work firstly towards the right. Work a whole stitch at the top of the diamond. Give the left-hand pair 2 twists, pin, cover the pin with whole stitch (Fig. 12).

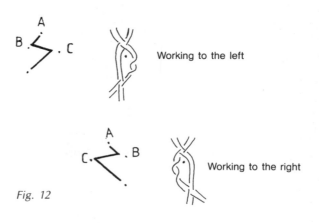

Working to the left

Working to the right

Fig. 12

The worker remains the same pair throughout and is twisted twice as it passes around each pin.

Work in whole stitch bringing in 1 pair at each pinhole until the widest point is reached; then 1 pair is left out at each pinhole until only 2 pairs remain at the last pinhole. Work whole stitch, 2 twists to the workers, pin, cover the pin with whole stitch. Give 1 twist to each of the left-out pairs from the diamond before passing the gimp through.

Curved headside and picots To work a curved headside, pairs must be left out when working the 'down' side, carried around the 'valley' and then brought in to the pattern again on the 'up' side. When working the down side and after the gimp, give 2 twists, whole stitch through the 2 headside passives, picot, then work back through the 2 headside passives and leave.

Each pinhole is worked in the same way.

When working the up side take the 3rd pair from the headside and work in whole stitch through the 2 passives, picot, then whole stitch back through the remaining headside pairs, twist twice, pass the gimp through and twist ready to work the next stitch.

The pairs in the valley are worked through each other in whole stitch.

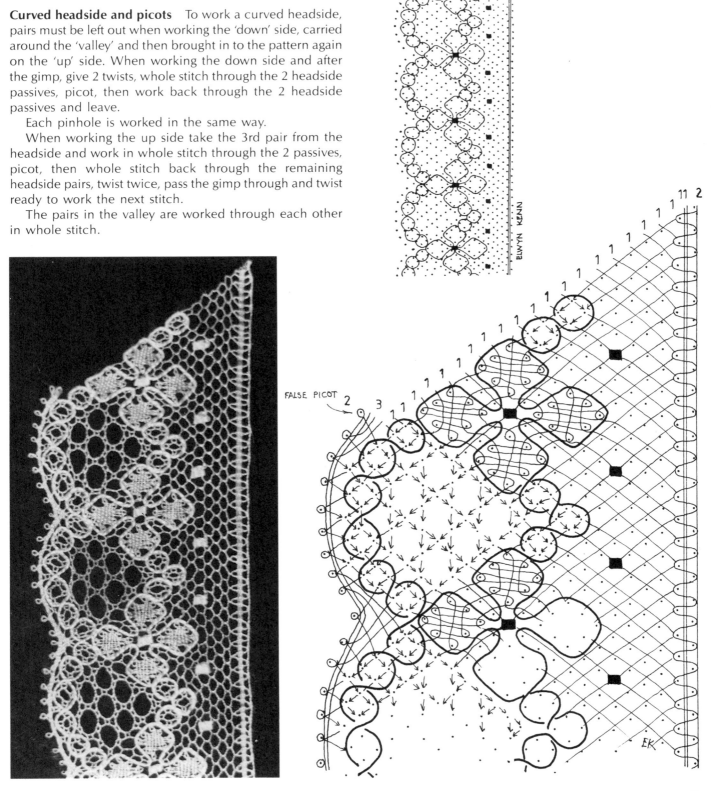

Geraldton Wax
Chamelaucium uncinatum

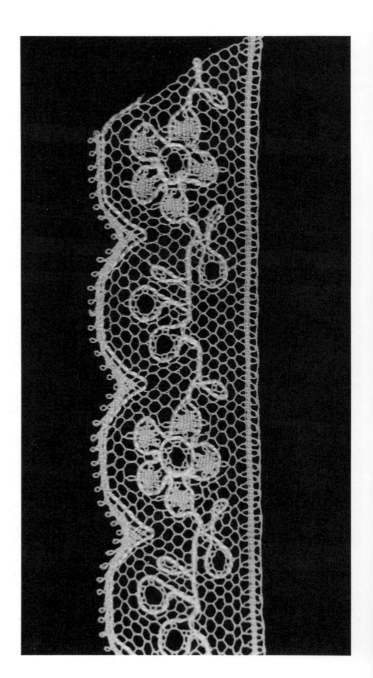

- 21 pairs—DMC or Madeira No. 50.
- 1 gimp pair and 1 single gimp bobbin—Perle No. 8.
- 1 extra gimp pair is needed for each pattern repeat.

Catchpin in the ground A catchpin is sometimes worked when the gimp thread is in a vertical line between the pattern feature and the ground, either to the left or to the right. In this pattern catchpin stitches are worked around the flowers.

Work in whole stitch to the first catchpin, do not twist the workers but pass the gimp through. Twist the workers 3 times. Put a pin to the left of this pair and work a ground stitch. The gimp is now passed through the left-hand pair, no twists, and worked in whole stitch to the next catchpin. Complete the petal in whole stitch.

Ending the gimps The small ring of gimp in the centre of each flower must be finished off. The gimps are crossed then taken back through at least 2 pairs on each side, if possible. Leave the gimp bobbins hanging at the back of the pillow to be cut off when the work has progressed (Fig. 13).

Fig. 13

Nook pins When working flowers nook pins are used to hold the gimp in place, thus forming the petals.

These are worked in various ways. In this pattern two methods are used:
A. Between the first and second petals a passive pair is taken out to form the nook pin. Twist 3 times, pin, pass the gimps through, then use this pair to work the first honeycomb stitch in the centre of the flower.
B. All the other nook pins are worked: 1 twist, whole stitch, pin, whole stitch, 1 twist is given to both pairs which then continue the pattern.

The number of twists given when working nook pins may be varied depending on the pattern being worked and the effect required.

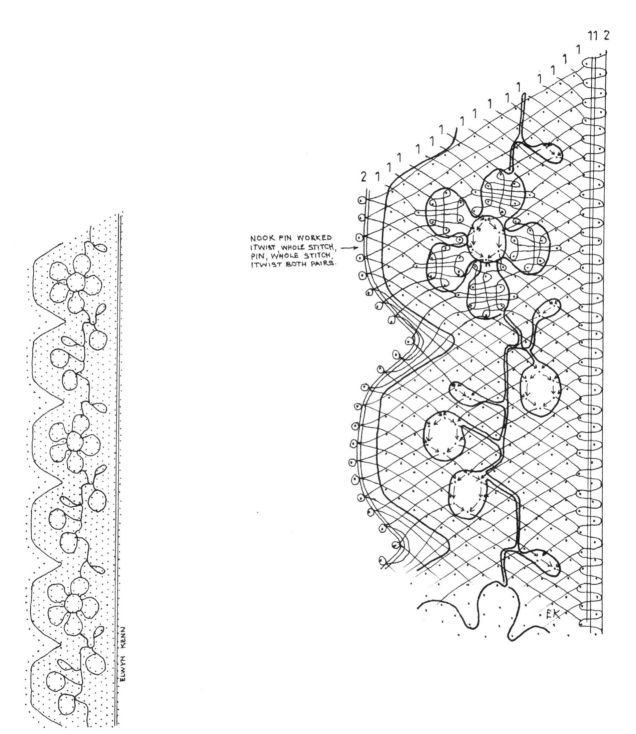

NOOK PIN WORKED
1TWIST, WHOLE STITCH,
PIN, WHOLE STITCH,
1TWIST BOTH PAIRS.

ELWYN KENN

EK

Rosy Baeckea
Baeckea ramosissima

- 20 pairs—Brok 100 or Madeira 'Tanne' No. 80.
- 2 extra pairs are added to each flower.
- 1 gimp pair—Perle No. 12.
- 1 extra gimp pair is needed for each pattern repeat.

Footside and honeycomb stitch Hang 2 pairs on A. Twist the pairs each side of this pin 3 times. Work a whole stitch then twist each pair 3 times. Hang 1 pair on each pin at B.

At A leave the right-hand pair, then with the left-hand pair work in whole stitch through the 2 passives from B. Twist the workers twice, ready to work the honeycomb stitch at C (Fig. 14). In this pattern the catchpin is worked as a honeycomb stitch.

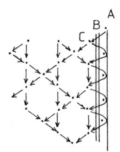

Fig. 14

Honeycomb ground is worked in diagonal rows, a long row from the footside followed by a short row. The short row can be worked in either direction. Continue to work honeycomb stitch in the direction of the arrows, working the catchpin as a honeycomb stitch and the footside in the usual way.

Adding extra pairs to the flowers When working the flowers extra pairs are needed to give fullness to the whole stitch. These pairs can be added over the workers or over the gimp.

I prefer to add the pairs over the gimp so that they lie in the correct position to fill any gaps in the whole stitch. This method also helps eliminate the small space between the gimp and the whole stitch created when added pairs are hung over the workers. Care must be taken to tension the gimp, keeping a smooth edge to the petals.

When a pair is no longer required it can be carried a little way with the gimp or headside passives, then discarded to be cut off later.

As the number of pairs added to the work depends on the thickness of the thread and the effect required, the diagrams in this book are for the thread stated. If the thread and the number of added pairs has been changed notes should be kept of the variations so that each flower can be repeated in the same manner.

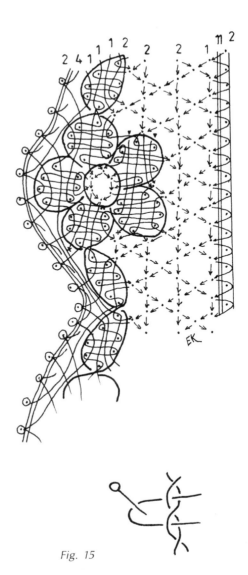

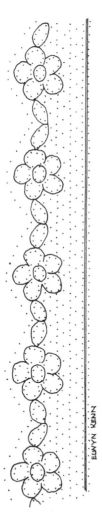

Fig. 15

There are no pinholes marked for the loops of gimp between the petals.

To work give 1 twist between the gimp loop of the petals. Place a pin to hold the gimp loop, as in Figure 15.

The Western Jewel
Hypochrysops halyaetus

- 18 pairs—Madeira 'Tanne' No. 80.
- 1 gimp pair and 1 single gimp bobbin—Perle.No. 12 or silver or gold thread.

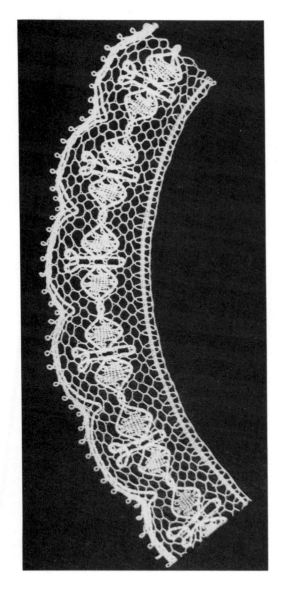

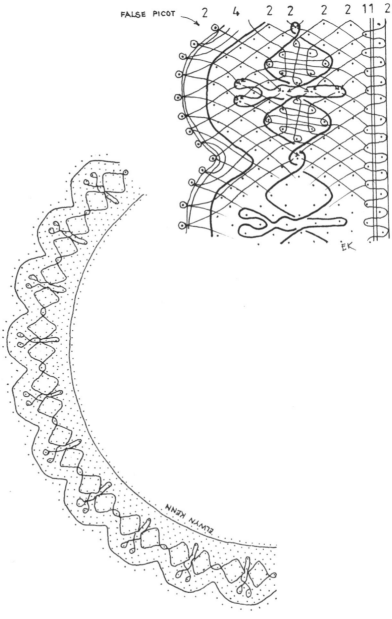

Gungurru
Eucalyptus caesia

- 18 pairs—Brok 120 or Madeira 'Tanne' No. 80.
- Gimps—Perle No. 12.

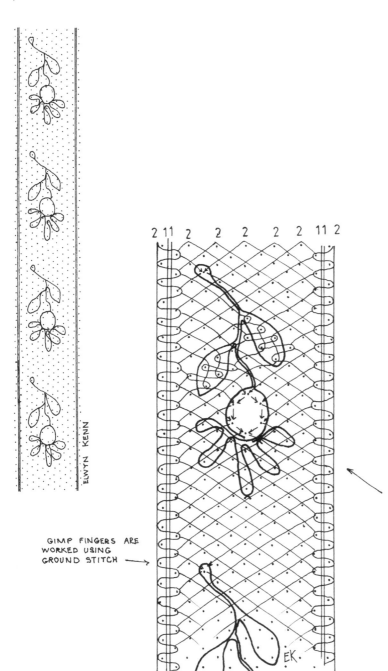

ELWYN KENN

2 11 2   2   2   2   2   11 2

GIMP FINGERS ARE
WORKED USING
GROUND STITCH →

EK.

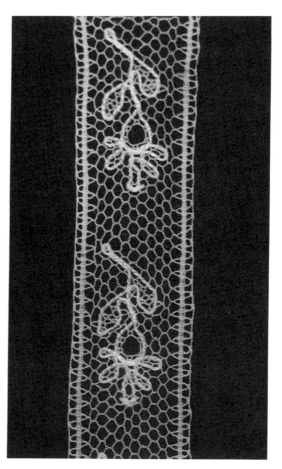

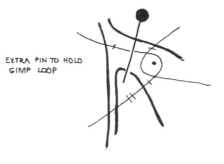

EXTRA PIN TO HOLD
GIMP LOOP

15

Cut-leaf Daisy

Brachycome multifida

Circular Motif

- 38 pairs—Brok 120 or Madeira 'Tanne' No. 80.
- 3 gimp pairs—Perle No. 12.

To begin a circle with a picot edge   Hang 2 pairs on a pin at A. Work a false picot.

Hang 4 pairs on a pin on the left-hand side of the pillow. Press the pin down to hold the threads firmly. Whole stitch the passive pairs through the pairs from pin A (Fig. 16).

Give 3 twists to the centre pairs. Put in the next pin to the right and add 2 pairs over the workers. Give 3 twists to each new pair (Fig. 17).

Continue toward the right, adding pairs as the diagram and working picots at edge.

For a wider edge add 6 instead of 4 pairs after the false picot.

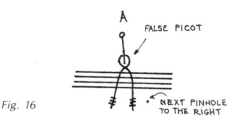

Fig. 16

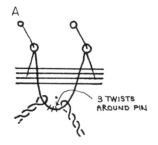

Fig. 17

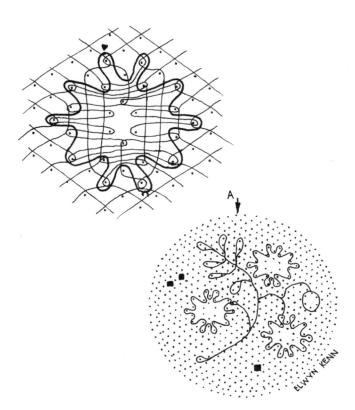

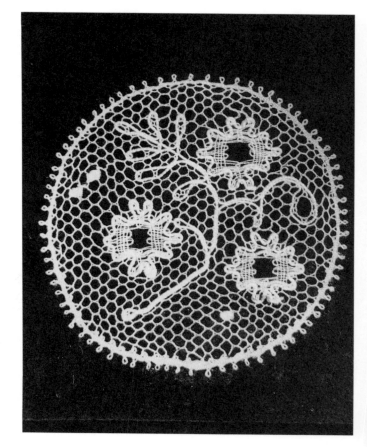

16

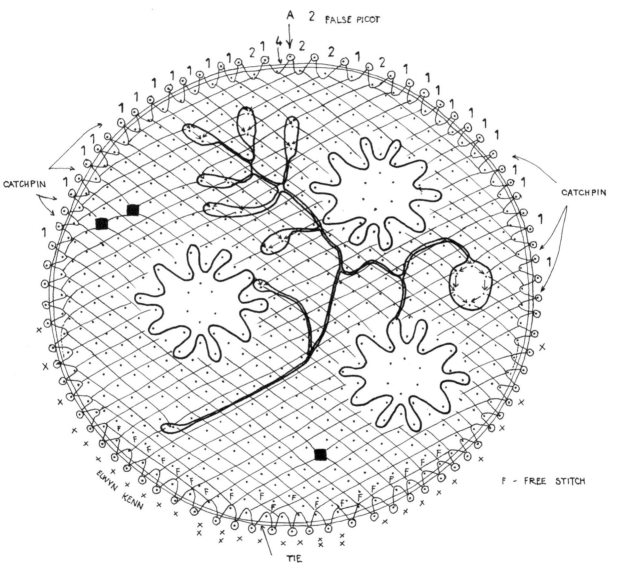

A 2 FALSE PICOT

CATCHPIN

CATCHPIN

ELWYN KENN

TIE

F - FREE STITCH

A *free stitch* is a ground stitch without a pin. It is worked where gaps may appear around a pattern feature or in this case along the lower edge of the circle where gaps may also occur.

Peach Blossom Tea Tree

Leptospermum squarrosum

Hexagonal motif

- 26 pairs—Brok 120 or Madeira 'Tanne' No. 80.
- 3 extra pairs are added to each flower.
- 1 extra pair is added at each centre pinhole.
- Gimps—Perle No. 12.

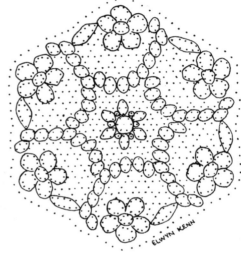

There are no pinholes marked for the loops of gimp between the petals.

For directions see Figure 15 on page 13.

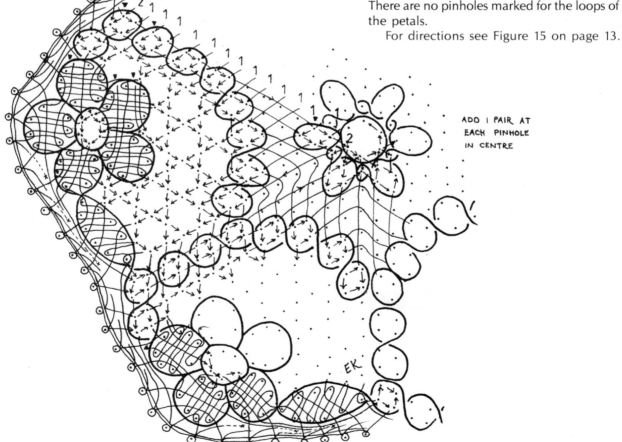

ADD 1 PAIR AT EACH PINHOLE IN CENTRE

FALSE PICOT

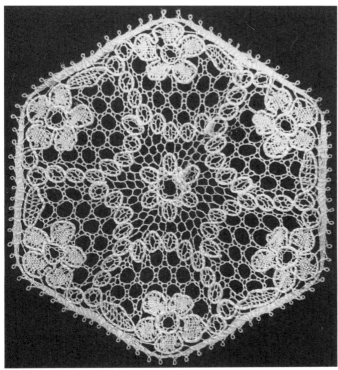

Edging

- 32 pairs—Brok 120 or Madeira 'Tanne' No. 80.
- 5 extra pairs are added to the flowers in each pattern repeat.
- Gimps—Perle No. 12.

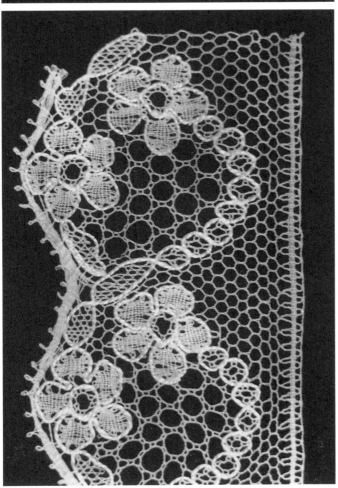

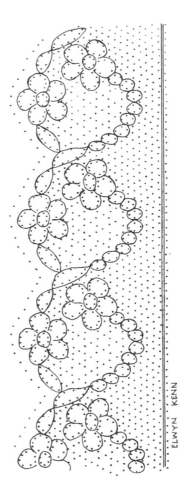

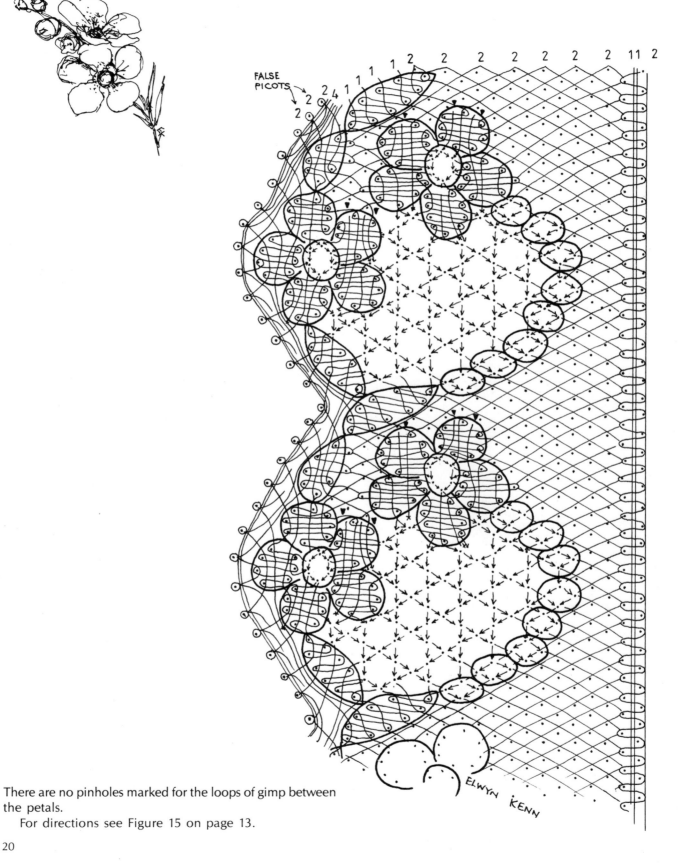

There are no pinholes marked for the loops of gimp between the petals.

For directions see Figure 15 on page 13.

Baby's mittens with Lillypilly lace

Apron with Geraldton Wax edging. Pricking was enlarged until suitable for Brillante d'Alsace No. 30 or Sylko No. 50

Cut-leaf Daisy—circular motif

Peach Blossom Tea Tree edging

Peach Blossom Tea Tree hexagonal motif

Ring box with Native Lasiandra lace

Amaryllis Azure mat

Spotted Sun Orchid—circular motif

Native Lasiandra
Melastoma affine

- 18 pairs—Brok 120.
- 1 gimp pair and 1 single gimp bobbin—Perle No. 12.

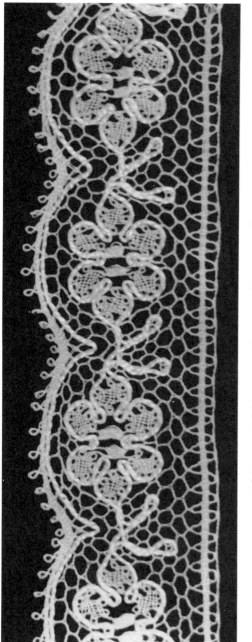

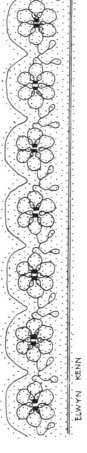

ELWYN KENN

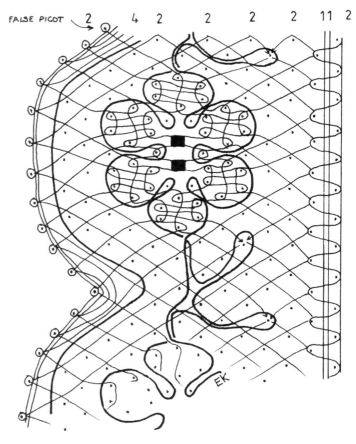

FALSE PICOT → 2   4   2   2   2   2   11 2

EK

Amaryllis Azure
Ogyris amaryllis

- 26 pairs—Brok 100 or 120.
- 1 extra pair is added at each centre pinhole.
- 2 gimp pairs and 2 single gimps—Perle No. 8.
- The wings are worked in a contrasting colour.

Adding a different coloured worker pair (Fig. 18). At the first pinhole at the top of the wing work a whole stitch and pin. Add coloured workers on a temporary pin to the left of the first pin. Both pairs from the whole stitch hang as passive pairs. Work 2 rows then remove the temporary pin.

At the last pinhole at the end of the wing, leave the coloured workers. Pin between the two remaining passives, then work a whole stitch with these two passives.

Tie the coloured workers three times and discard to the back of the pillow, to be cut off later.

Fig. 18   ADDING A DIFFERENT
COLOURED WORKER PAIR

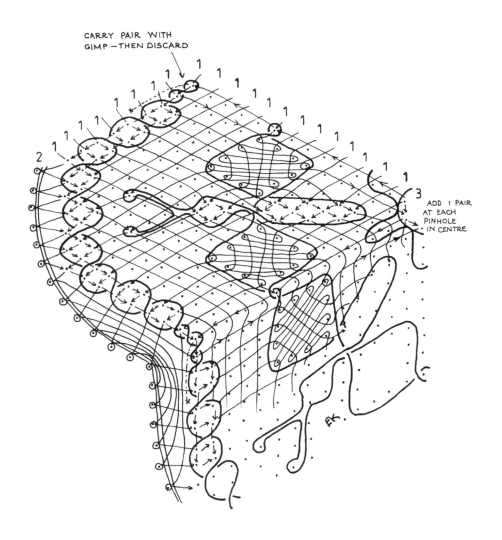

CARRY PAIR WITH
GIMP – THEN DISCARD

ADD 1 PAIR
AT EACH
PINHOLE
IN CENTRE

Fairy Wax Flower
Eriostemon verrucosus

- 21 pairs—Brok 100 or Madeira 'Tanne' No. 80.
- 3 gimp pairs—Perle No. 12.
- 1 extra gimp pair is needed for each pattern repeat.

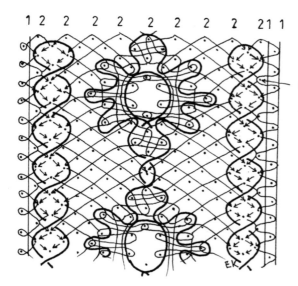

WORK AS A CATCHPIN

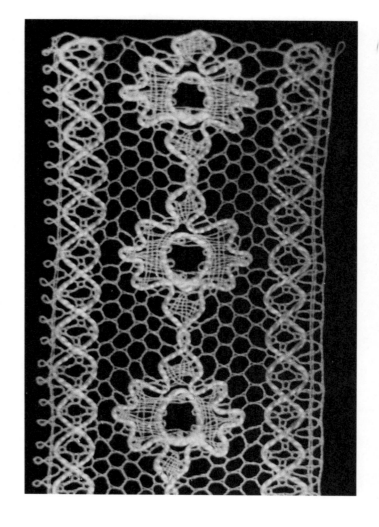

ELWYN KENN

Spotted Sun Orchid

Thelymitra ixioides

Insertion

- 22 pairs—Brok 120 or Madeira 'Tanne' No. 80.
- 3 extra pairs are added to each flower.
- 1 gimp pair and 2 single gimp bobbins—Perle No. 12.
- 1 extra gimp pair is needed for each flower centre.

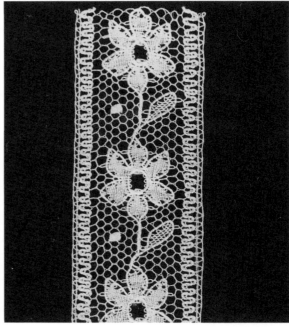

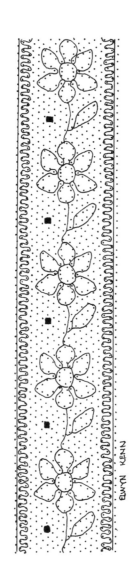

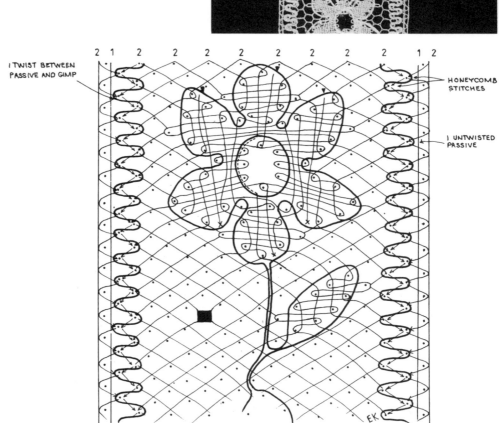

I TWIST BETWEEN PASSIVE AND GIMP

HONEYCOMB STITCHES

I UNTWISTED PASSIVE

2 1 2 2 2 2 2 2 2 2 2 1 2

ELWYN KENN

EK

Circular motif

- 44 pairs—Brok 120 or Madeira 'Tanne' No. 80.
- 3 gimp pairs—Perle No. 12.

To begin a circle Hang 4 pairs on pin A (Fig. 19).

Work a whole stitch with the 2 left-hand pairs, then give 3 twists to all 4 pairs. Hang 4 pairs on a pin on the left-hand side of the pillow. Press the pin down to hold the threads firmly. Whole stitch the passive pairs through the 2 centre pairs from pin A (Fig. 20).

Give 3 twists to the centre pairs. Put in the next pin to the right and add 2 pairs over the workers. Give 3 twists to each new pair (Fig. 21).

Continue toward the right, adding pairs as the diagram.

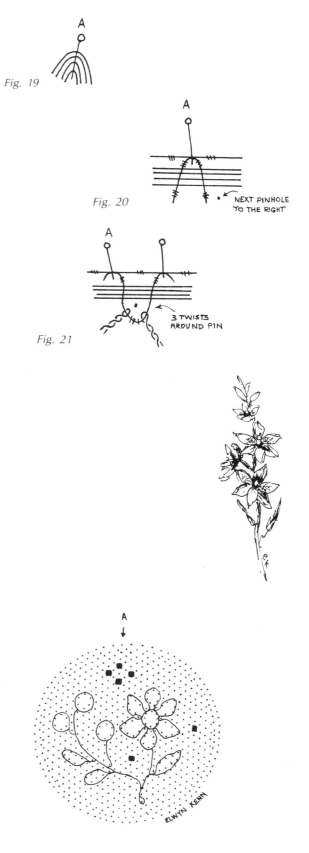

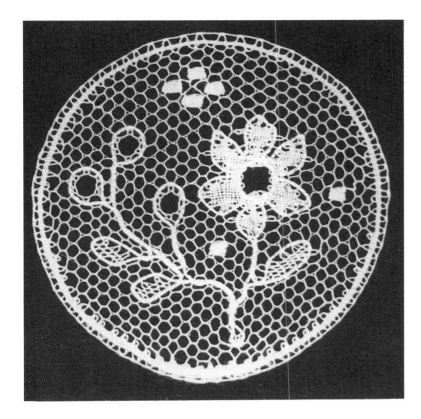

31

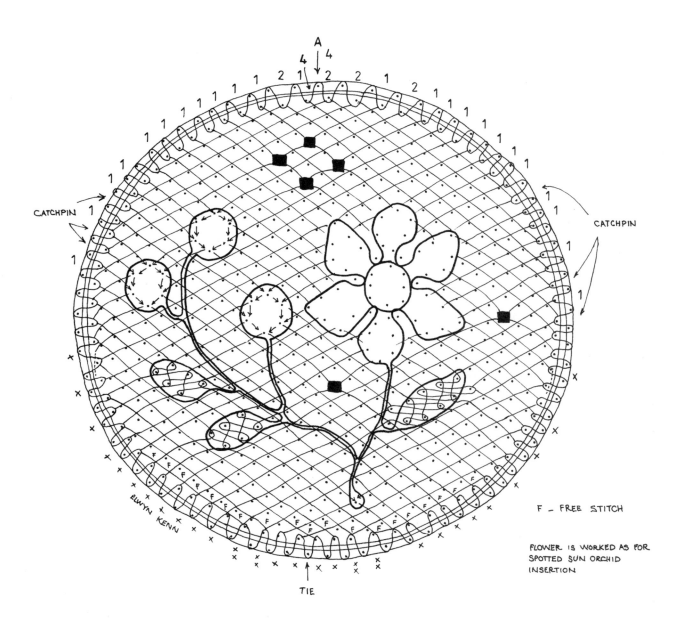

CATCHPIN

CATCHPIN

ELWYN KENN

F — FREE STITCH

FLOWER IS WORKED AS FOR
SPOTTED SUN ORCHID
INSERTION

TIE

Bower Plant
Pandorea jasminoides

- 42 pairs—Brok 100 or 120.
- 4 extra pairs are added in each section of the hexagonal mat.
- 1 extra pair is added at each pinhole in the centre.
- Gimps—Perle No. 12.

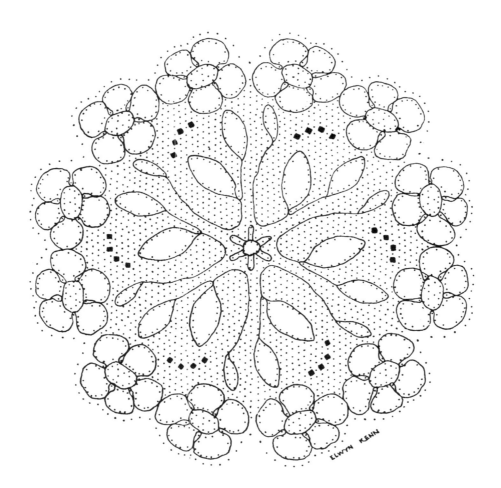

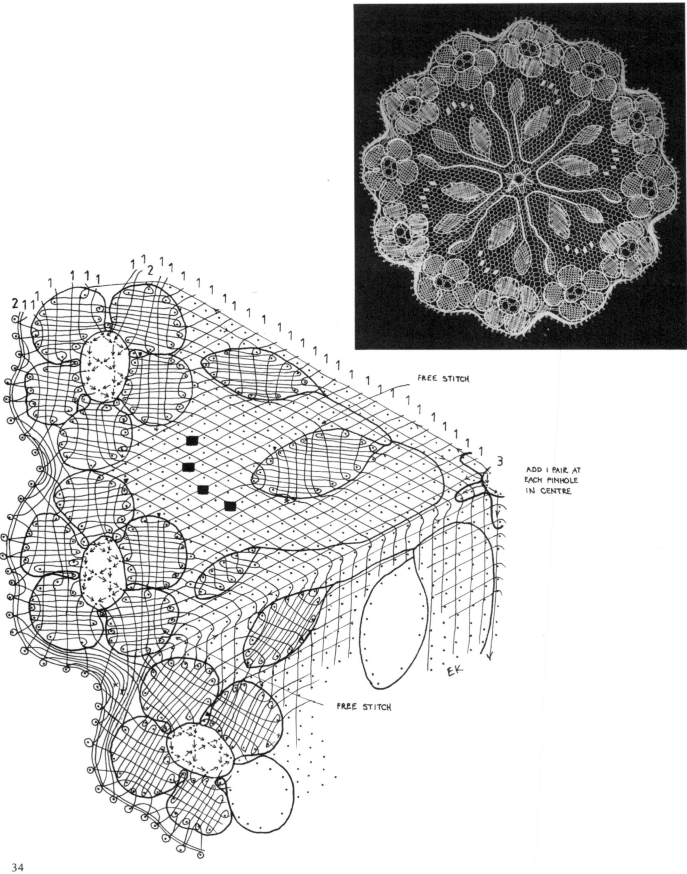

FREE STITCH

ADD 1 PAIR AT
EACH PINHOLE
IN CENTRE

FREE STITCH

EK

34

Grampians Bauera

Bauera sessiliflora

- Approx. 39 pairs—Brok 120 or Madeira 'Tanne' No. 80.
- Extra pairs are added to work the corner.
- Gimps—Perle No. 12.

Diagram 1

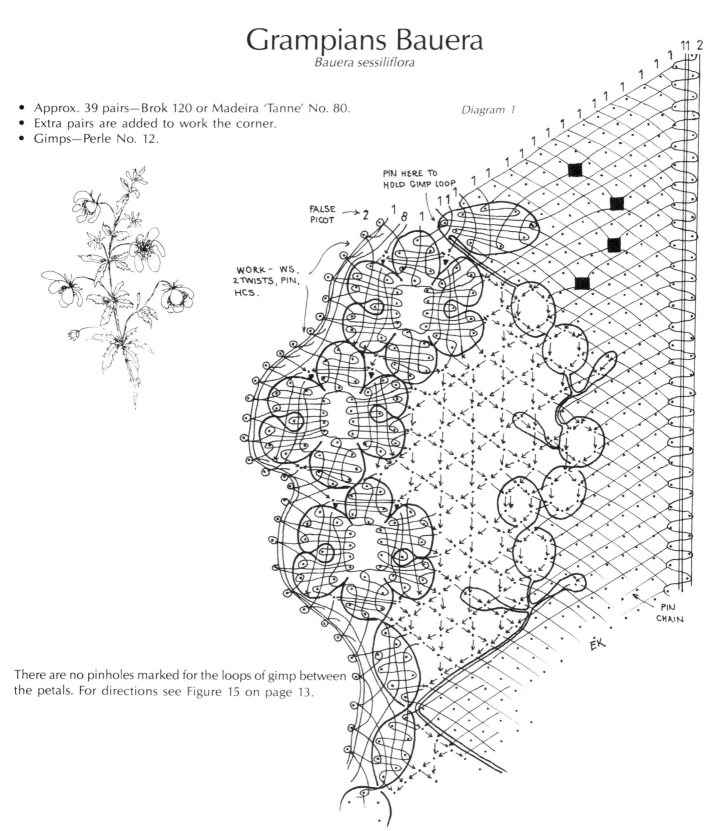

There are no pinholes marked for the loops of gimp between the petals. For directions see Figure 15 on page 13.

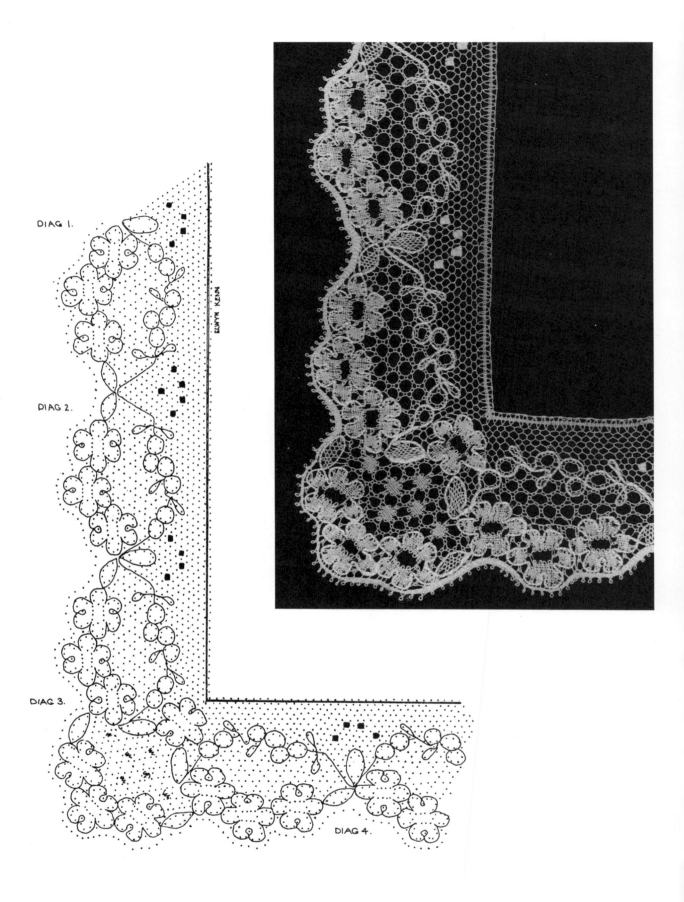

DIAG 1.

DIAG 2.

DIAG 3.

DIAG 4.

ELWYN KENN

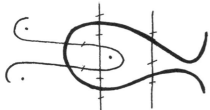

TO WORK THE
NOOK PINS

Diagram 2

EK·

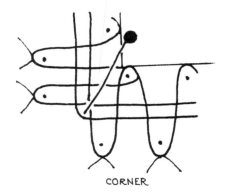

CORNER

Diagram 3

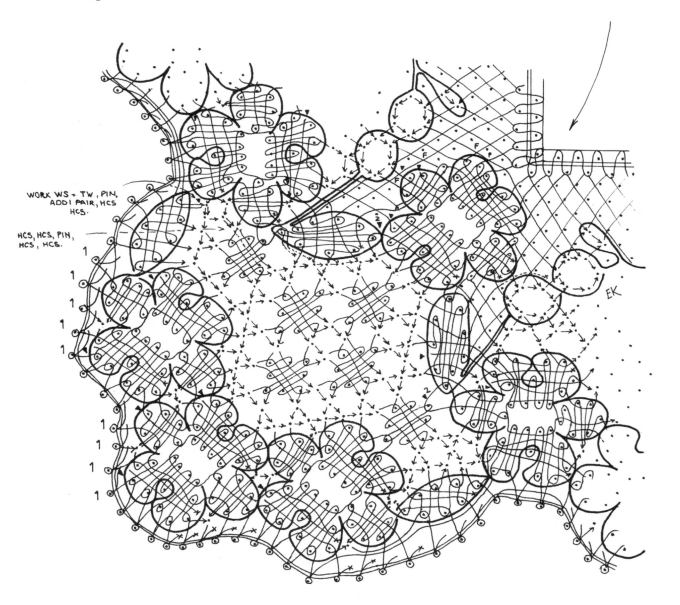

WORK WS + TW, PIN,
ADD1 PAIR, HCS
HCS.

HCS, HCS, PIN,
HCS, HCS.   1

1

1

1

1

1

1

1

EK

38

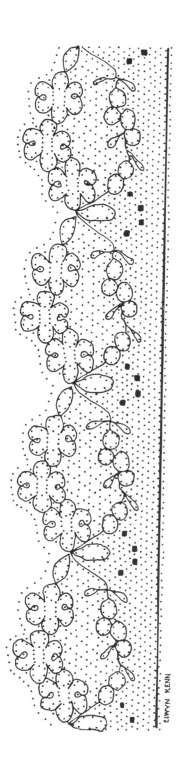

Grampians Bauera edging

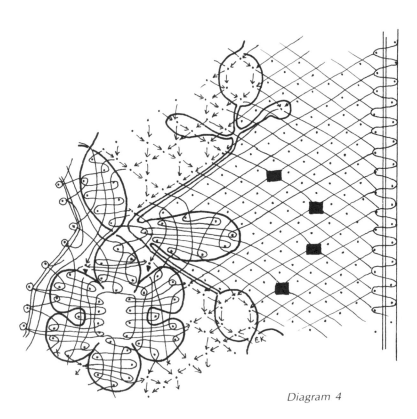

Diagram 4

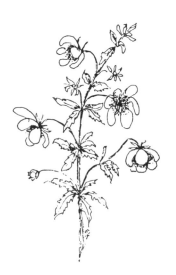

Karkalla
Carpobrotus rossii

- 22 pairs—Brok 120.
- 1 extra pair is added to each flower.
- Gimps—Perle No. 12.

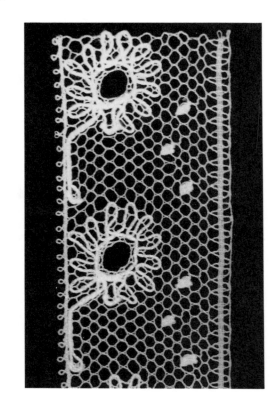

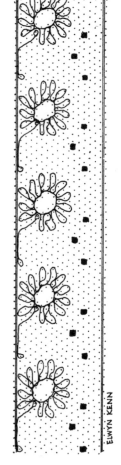

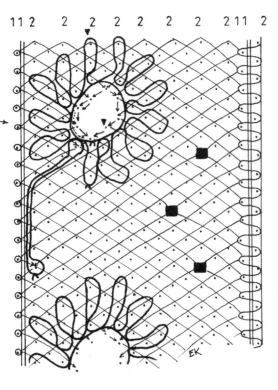

CARRY 1 PAIR WITH
GIMP AND DISCARD →

Coastal Tea Tree

Leptospermum laevigatum

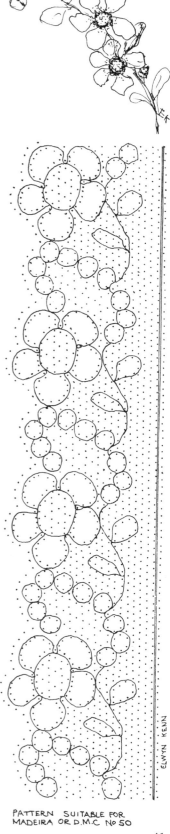

Edging

- 34 pairs—Brok 120 or Madiera 'Tanne' No. 80.
- 5 extra pairs are added to each flower.
- 2 gimp pairs—Perle No. 12.
- 2 extra gimp pairs are needed for each pattern repeat.

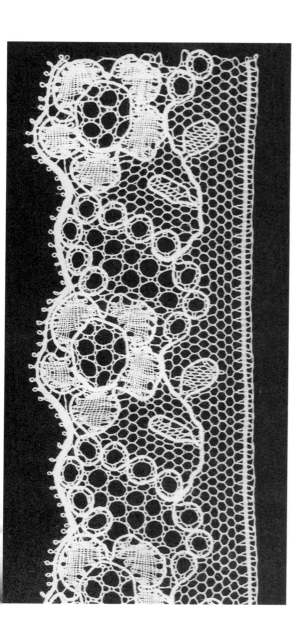

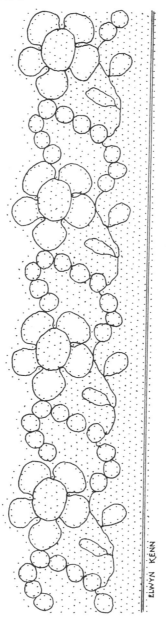

PATTERN SUITABLE FOR
MADEIRA OR D.M.C No 50

ELWYN KENN

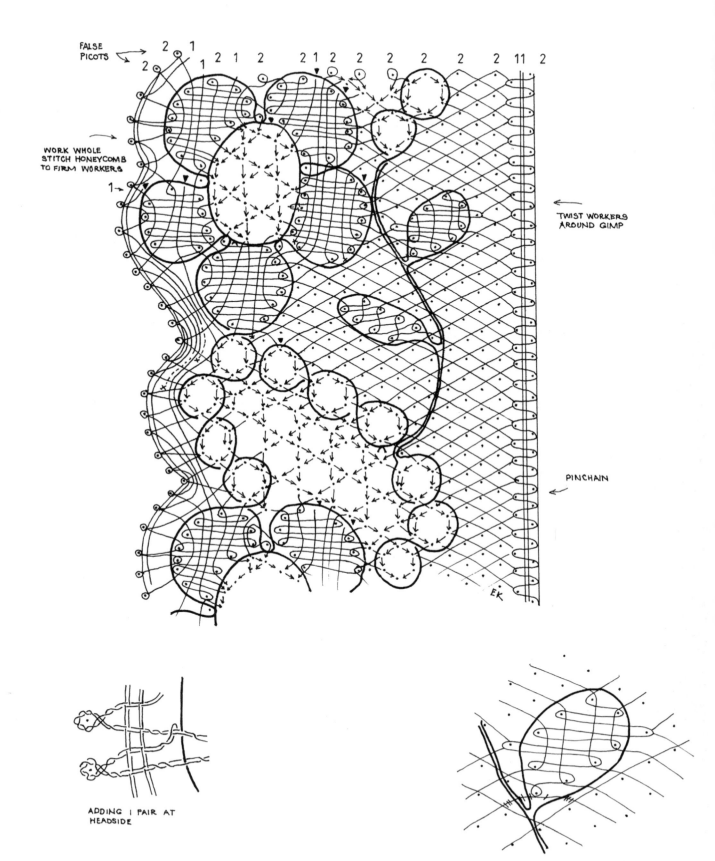

FALSE
PICOTS

2 1
2

1 2 1 2   2 1 2   2   2   2   2 11 2

WORK WHOLE
STITCH HONEYCOMB
TO FIRM WORKERS

1

TWIST WORKERS
AROUND GIMP

PINCHAIN

EK

ADDING 1 PAIR AT
HEADSIDE

DIAGRAM FOR WORKING FIRST LEAF

Hexagonal mat

- 30 pairs—Brok 120 or Madeira 'Tanne' No. 80.
- 5 extra pairs are added to each flower.
- 2 gimp pairs—Perle No. 12.
- 2 extra gimp pairs are needed for each pattern repeat.

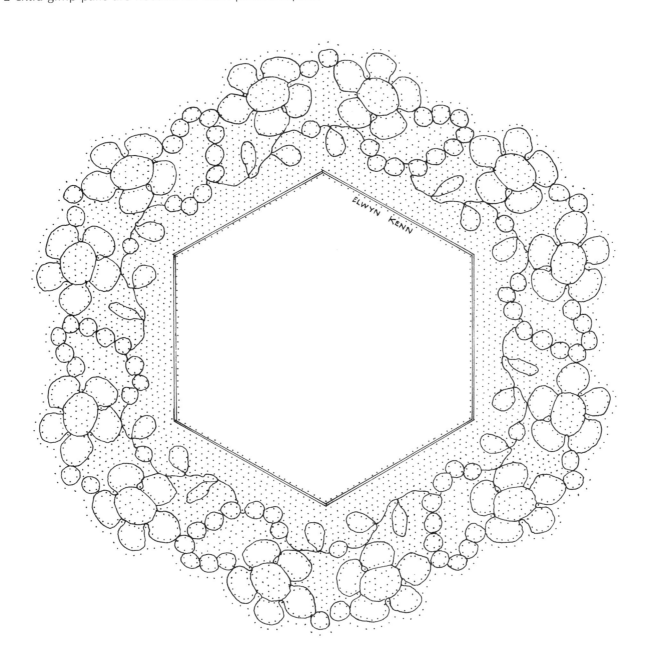

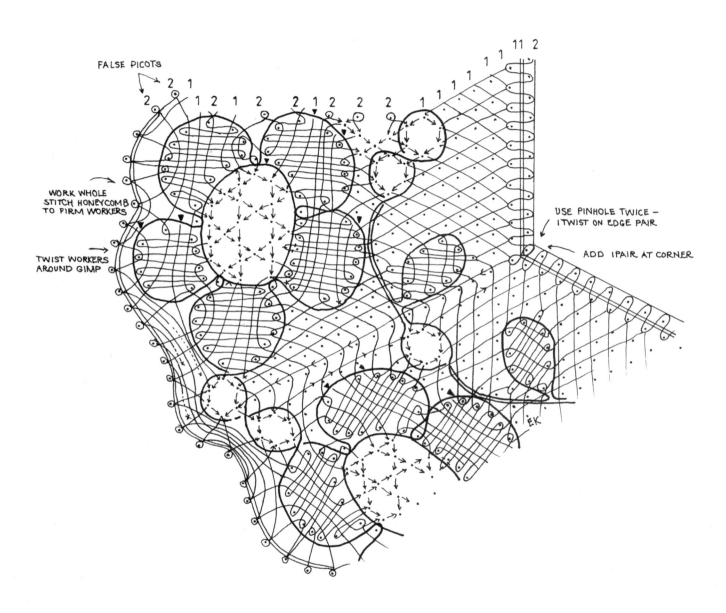

FALSE PICOTS

WORK WHOLE
STITCH HONEYCOMB
TO FIRM WORKERS

TWIST WORKERS
AROUND GIMP

USE PINHOLE TWICE —
1 TWIST ON EDGE PAIR

ADD 1 PAIR AT CORNER

EK